YOU CAN CHANGE HOW YOU FEEL:
A Rational-Emotive Approach

by
Gerald Kranzler
Counseling Department
University of Oregon

RESOURCE *Publications* • Eugene, Oregon

Resource Publications
A division of Wipf and Stock Publishers
199 W 8th Ave. Suite 3
Eugene. OR 97401

You Can Change How You Feel
By Kranzler, Gerald
Copyright©1974 by Kranzler. Gerald
ISBN 13: 978-1-5326-6833-3
Publication date 9/10/2018
Previously published by Gerald D. Kranzler. 1974

CONTENTS

PREFACE

The purpose of this booklet is to introduce you to some principles and techniques that may be useful to you in solving your personal problems. Most of the material is based directly or indirectly on the pioneering work of Dr. Albert Ellis, a psychologist who is best known for developing the approach to psychotherapy called Rational-Emotive Therapy (RET). A list of some of his better-known books may be found in the Bibliography.

I first became interested in RET in 1963 when I was a graduate student in counseling psychology. The ideas made a lot of sense to me personally, and their application to my own problems of that time helped me significantly. Unfortunately, perhaps because I often fail to think as creatively as I would like, I had great difficulty in teaching these ideas to clients with whom I was counseling and to students whom I was teaching at the university.

Fortunately for me, I had an advisee, Stan Laughridge, who went beyond my own knowledge of RET by attending workshops taught by Ellis, by reading materials written by other RET therapists, and by doing RET with clients in various settings. When he taught a course in RET one summer, I enrolled in it, and for the first time learned how the basic ideas could be taught quickly and simply to almost anyone. (Since then Stan has earned his Ph.D. and currently is director of a mental health clinic.)

I taught my first RET seminar at the University of Oregon in the early 1970's, and since then have offered it almost every term. The materials included in this booklet are those that have seemed to be most helpful to students in learning how to apply RET principles to their own lives and to the process of helping others.

An earlier version of this booklet was used by many students in my classes, and several of them subsequently used it with their clients. While most of them had suggestions for minor changes in the booklet, their comments about its effectiveness were most encouraging.

A number of other persons helped improve the original version. Grateful acknowledgment is made to Dr. Albert Ellis, Dr. Stanley Laughridge, Dr. Maxie Maultsby, Sandy Harris, Stan Hultgren, and the many others who read the original draft and made valuable suggestions; to Suzi Prichard, who typed the first draft and made helpful comments along the way; and to Carolyn, who encouraged me to write it, and on account of whom I smile a lot.

I. INTRODUCTION

The material in this booklet is based on the assumption that it is possible to learn something useful about the feelings you have: that you can learn to understand **why** you feel as you do, and to understand **how** to change or control your extreme negative feelings of anger, anxiety, or depression.

I agree with the psychologists Ellis and Harper (1973) when they contend that:

> "Today, after inventing eyeglasses, radar, electronic calculators, and other perceiving—moving—thinking aids, he (man) rules supreme on this earth and is literally seeking other worlds to conquer . . . Only in the emotional area has man as yet made remarkably few advances. In spite of amazing progress in other areas, he is still not appreciably more emotionally mature, stable, and happy than he was in past centuries. Indeed, he is in some ways more childish, emotionally uncontrolled, and mentally ill than ever." (p. 18)

How successful has your own emotional education been? Ask yourself the questions listed below. Affirmative replies may mean that you could benefit from some additional learning:

1. Are you excessively concerned about the love and approval of others? Do you feel anxious or depressed when you learn that others do not like you? Do you often spend so much time trying to please everyone else that you have little time or energy left to get what you want out of life? Do you feel unlovable when no one seems to love you?

2. Are you excessively concerned with doing well at everything you do? Do you feel upset when you fail at something you want to accomplish? Do you avoid doing things that might be fun because you might do so poorly that others would criticize you or laugh at you? Do you feel worthless when you are not successful?

3. Do you feel angry at others when they do things you consider to be bad or wicked? Do you feel upset when someone who commits a crime is not punished? Do you frequently criticize and verbally or physically attack others who do or say things that seem stupid or wicked?

4. Do you feel depressed, guilty, or sinful about some things you have done in the past? Do you still feel upset about some things that happened to you as a child?
5. Do you often worry about death or an accident or something else that might happen to you in the future? Do you sometimes worry so much that you get sick? Are you afraid of many things, such as dogs, snakes, insects, other people, taking tests, riding in airplanes, or speaking in front of groups?
6. Do you often feel helpless and at the mercy of other people and events? Do you often feel frustrated and powerless to do what you really want to do?
7. Do you often feel listless and bored, unable to do your work or get any fun out of life? Do you sometimes put more effort into avoiding a job you don't like than the job itself would take? Do you put off unpleasant tasks as long as possible?
8. Do you feel incapable of making your own decisions? Do you frequently ask people for advice? Do you feel dependent on someone or something else to take care of you?
9. Do you spend a lot of time worrying about other people's problems? Do you feel upset when someone close to you has something bad happen to them? Are you outraged at the injustices prevalent in our society?

Ellis' thesis, and the thesis of this manual, is that emotional and behavioral problems such as these may be a result of irrational thinking, and that we can change such feelings by changing what we think.

Very likely you are able to control most of your own activities. You decide whether you wish to run or walk, or whether to go to school or to the store. You may even make long-range decisions about your activities, such as planning to take a trip to the beach for the weekend, and then carry out your plans. You may have difficulty changing some behaviors such as overeating or smoking, but generally speaking you can control most of what you do.

You are also able to control your thoughts to a great extent. Even though you may "find yourself" thinking about your trip to the beach, you can change what you are thinking and concentrate, instead, on preparing a menu for tonight's dinner or on correcting your students' arithmetic papers.

Your feelings, on the other hand, seem to have a life of their own. You may **wish** to feel calm when you talk to someone you don't like, but you feel very angry nevertheless. Nor does it seem that you can keep yourself from becoming afraid just by deciding not to be afraid. It seems to you that your feelings are spontaneous responses to people or events over which you have little or no control.

It may seem to you that psychological pain is caused in much the same way as physical pain. Your theory may be diagramed as follows:

A (Activating Event)	causes	C (Consequences)
Being poked with a pin	causes	Physical Pain
Being called a name	causes	Psychological Pain (e.g., anger)

That is, you believe that you have no more choice about feeling anger at point C when someone calls you a name than you do about feeling pain at point C when you are poked with a pin.

If your theory about emotional pain were true, that is, if someone calling you a name really could cause you to become angry, then it would seem that you have only two choices: (1) experience the anger, and **express** it, for example, by calling the other person a name back, or (2) experience the anger and **suppress** it, for example, by pretending that you're not angry at all or maybe even that you enjoy being called that name.

If you really had only two choices, then most psychologists would agree that expressing your anger usually would be better for your long-term psychological well-being than suppressing it. Most people agree that "bottling up" your emotions is not psychologically healthy in the long run.

Fortunately for all of us, you have a third choice, which is **not to experience the emotion at all** or at least not to have the feeling in an intense form. Someone can call you a name at Point A and you needn't feel anger at Point C. In order to understand how that is possible, it will first be necessary to understand what emotions are and why we feel as we do.

II. EMOTIONS AS PROBLEMS

Have you ever done something so foolish that you later wondered how you could have done such a thing? Have you ever become so excited while giving a speech or taking a test that you forgot material you knew well? Have you ever been so angry at someone that you could not get to sleep at night, only to discover later that it wasn't as serious as you had thought? Very likely you have done all of these things. If so, you have experienced the debilitating effects of intense emotional arousal.

Emotions may be thought of as having two parts or phases: (1) intensified **feelings** about a situation, and (2) a pattern of physiological changes in the body. Physiological changes vary according to the intensity of the feelings. When feelings are mild, the physiological changes are small. When you feel mild annoyance or irritation, for example, the changes include increases in digestive functions, pulse rate, blood pressure, and rate of breathing; you are "keyed up"; you have energy to work harder and longer and are more able to change the frustrating situation you are in.

When your feelings are strong, however, the accompanying physiological changes are extensive. In strong fear or anger the adrenal glands release adrenaline into the bloodstream, stimulating the heart to greater activity. The circulatory system begins to take blood from the stomach and intestines and send it to the big muscles of your arms and legs. The liver pumps glycogen into your bloodstream, providing you with a quick source of extra energy. Your rate of breathing increases, your eyes dilate, your hair bristles. Your body is on full emergency status and you are physiologically ready to run or fight.

In intense grief or despair the physiological changes are somewhat different. There is a general reduction of pulse rate, breathing, and muscular strength, there is a general numbness of the body as if to make it easier to bear the blows. Whereas anger or fear summon reserves of energy, grief or depression result in a tired state.

When mild, emotions may help you to achieve what you wish to do. In mild feelings of anxiety, for example, concomitant physiological changes increase mental alertness. You can, therefore, study longer and more effectively when you are a bit afraid that you may not get the grades you want. You can usually make a better speech when you are somewhat concerned about how it will be received, because you then put forth more effort in both preparation and delivery of the speech.

Strong emotions such as intense fears or rage, however, are about as useful as matches in a dynamite factory. They prevent you from behaving rationally in at least two ways. First, under the influence of intense, negative emotions you are unable to concentrate on the problem. Students who are extremely fearful of failing an examination are unable to concentrate either while preparing for the exam or while taking it. The sufferer from stage fright is so worried and tense that he stutters and stammers and forgets the words he wants to say.

Second, under strong emotional arousal you have an urge to do something, even if it's not in your long-term self-interest. You will tend to act first and think about the consequences of your act later, rather than planning a rational solution to the problem.

Intense emotional reactions may have been more functional at an earlier stage of man's development, when he (or she) was faced with frequent physical dangers. When being attacked by a roaring lion or a hostile enemy, ability to exert great amounts of energy in either flight or fight was useful.

Living in a modern society as you do, your emergencies are more likely to result from social or psychological than from physical threats. Instead of wild animals you are faced with failing in important life tasks or with losing social status. It makes no difference to your body whether your threat is a wild animal or giving a speech. If your threat is interpreted as serious, your body puts into effect its inherited patterns of response—it prepares for strenuous **physical** action. But rational problem-solving in a modern world requires calm thinking—not high blood pressure, rapid breathing, and dilated eyes!

Thus, the more intense the emotion, the more it interferes with your being able to get what you want out of life. Mild emotions such as mild anxiety, irritation, and annoyance stimulate your efforts to solve the problem or to make reasonable preparations for the future: that is, they often are **facilitative**. Intense emotions, however, interfere with adjustment. When you experience intense unpleasant emotions, you are likely to be so concerned with relieving the immediate pain that you are unable to do what is best for you in the long run: that is, intense, sustained emotions tend to be **debilitative**.

Perhaps it should be stated over and over again that there is nothing wrong with having and expressing emotions! The idea of coldly going through life, machine-like, doesn't appeal to any of us. For most of us it is our emotions that make life fun, that give it a richness that makes life worth living. It is perfectly **normal** to have and express all kinds of emotions!

Usually you don't consider your feelings to be problems unless they are seen as inappropriate in intensity or duration. It is natural, for example, to be annoyed when someone interrupts while you are talking, but it becomes a problem to you (and perhaps others) if you become so angry that you forget what you were going to say or if it interferes with your work the rest of the day. It seems perfectly normal to be sad when one of your parents dies, but if you are still so depressed about it two years later that you can't get any enjoyment from life, you might be considered to have a problem.

What should you do if you have an emotional problem? When you have a legal problem, you take it to a lawyer. When your car develops mechanical problems, you probably take it to a mechanic. Why not take your emotional problems to someone trained to deal with them, too?

Unfortunately, in our society there still is a stigma attached to going to an expert for counseling or psychotherapy. You may be perfectly willing to tell anyone about your physical ailments, but you would rather be caught dead than be seen entering a counselor's or therapist's office.

More and more people are coming to realize that modern living is exceedingly complex and difficult, and that they are in many cases too close to their own emotional problems to view them objectively. They need also to realize that there is nothing to be ashamed of in admitting that they may need help. In fact, such an admission may be an indication of strength. Therefore, if you have emotional problems of concern to you, you would be wise to take them to a professional counselor.

The materials presented in the next few chapters were written with the intent of helping you to become your own counselor. It is assumed that they will be most helpful when used in conjunction with professional counseling. However, the materials may be of benefit to you even if you currently are not receiving counseling, especially if your problems are not too severe.

III. THINKING AND EMOTIONS

In the first century A.D., Epictetus, the Greek Stoic philosopher, wrote in the *Enchiridon* that "Men are disturbed not by things but the views they take of them." Shakespeare expressed a similar thought in *Hamlet*: "There is nothing good or bad but thinking makes it so." Montaigne, a modern French philosopher, said that "A man is hurt not so much by what happens, as by his opinion of what happens." The thesis of this manual is that your emotional problems are caused by your thinking. More specifically, your extreme, negative emotions are due largely to your irrational or illogical beliefs.

Recall the diagram presented in the introduction to this manual:

A (Activating Event)   **C (Consequences)**

causes

This diagram is quite accurate when representing physical pain: being stuck with a pin (A) really does cause pain (C). But the diagram is not accurate when representing psychological pain. It is **not** A (for example, someone calling you a name) that causes C (for example, anger), it is B, your Beliefs about being called names at point A, that causes you to feel anger at point C.

An example by Ellis (1969) might help to clarify this point. Suppose you pass by your friend's house and he sticks his head out the window and calls you all the nasty names he can think of. Let us also suppose that you become quite upset and angry at him. Now, instead, imagine that the building you pass by is a mental hospital, that you know your friend is an inmate there, and he sticks his head out the window and calls you those same vile names. Would you feel as upset and angry about the names he was calling you now as if he were "normal" and in his own house? Very likely not.

The Activating Event (being called names) was identical in both cases, but your feelings at point C were very different because you were saying something very different to yourself at point B. In the first case you probably were saying things like, "He shouldn't call me those rotten names! That's really terrible! I'll fix his wagon!" On the other hand, in the second case you might be telling yourself something like, "Poor, sick person. He can't help behaving crazily. Perhaps when he gets better he no longer will call me those names." Instead of anger, perhaps you would feel another emotion such as pity.

As I sit here writing this it is October in Oregon and it is raining quite steadily outside. I feel very pleased about that because I am telling myself "Good, that means it's probably snowing in the mountains, so we'll probably be able to start skiing soon." However, I know many people living in Oregon who are quite depressed when it begins raining in the Fall, usually because they are saying things like, "This is awful! Now it's going to rain practically non-stop for six months and I just can't stand gloomy weather!" Clearly, it is not the rain that causes depression: it is what we **think** about the rain that causes us to feel as we do.

Again, it is not A (the Activating Event) that is causing C (the emotional Consequence), it is B, your Beliefs about A, that causes C. Here is how my Oregon October Rain example would look in the diagram:

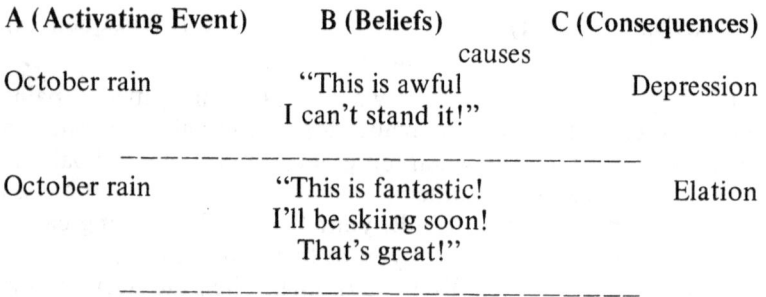

A (Activating Event)	B (Beliefs)	C (Consequences)
	causes	
October rain	"This is awful I can't stand it!"	Depression
	───────────────────	
October rain	"This is fantastic! I'll be skiing soon! That's great!"	Elation

The October rain at point A is the same, obviously, for both persons, so it couldn't be the rain that caused them to feel the opposite emotions of depression and elation at point C; it must have been their beliefs, that is, what they were **thinking**, at point B, that caused them to feel differently.

In the human being, thinking occurs largely in the form of self-verbalizations, that is, in the form of talking to yourself. When something happens at point A, you **talk to yourself** at point B, and this in turn causes an emotional response at point C. Mary says to Jim at point A, "I love you Jim!"; Jim says to himself at point B, "Fantastic! This is really great! What a lucky guy I am!" and at point C he feels joy or elation. On the other hand, suppose that at point B Jim says to himself, "Good God! This is awful! What I really wanted was to break off with Mary because I like Sally better. Now I'm really going to have to hurt Mary's feelings. It's really terrible how I've led her on without letting her know how I feel." In this case Jim certainly would not feel either joy or elation at point C. More likely he would be angry at himself or guilty, or depressed, and he might feel sorry for Mary. He would literally **think himself into** a disturbed condition.

The process by which you create your own emotional responses may be diagramed as follows:

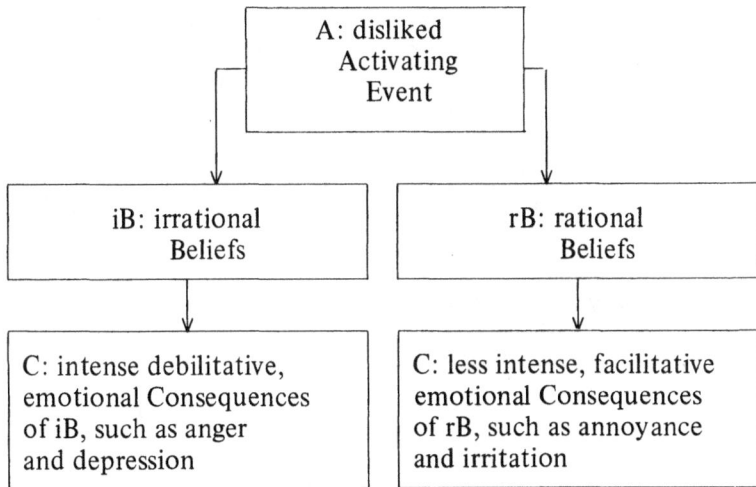

```
              ┌─────────────────┐
              │   A: disliked   │
              │   Activating    │
              │     Event       │
              └────────┬────────┘
        ┌──────────────┴──────────────┐
        ▼                             ▼
┌─────────────────┐         ┌─────────────────┐
│  iB: irrational │         │   rB: rational  │
│     Beliefs     │         │     Beliefs     │
└────────┬────────┘         └────────┬────────┘
         ▼                           ▼
┌──────────────────────┐   ┌──────────────────────┐
│ C: intense debilitat-│   │ C: less intense,     │
│ ive, emotional Conse-│   │ facilitative         │
│ quences of iB, such  │   │ emotional Conse-     │
│ as anger and         │   │ quences of rB, such  │
│ depression           │   │ as annoyance and     │
│                      │   │ irritation           │
└──────────────────────┘   └──────────────────────┘
```

If you have irrational beliefs (iB) about the Activating Event (A), then you will tend to upset yourself (C) to the extent that your emotions interfere with your self-interest (that is, your emotions are debilitative). If you are about to take a test on which you may fail (A), and if you tell yourself how **awful** and **terrible** failure would be and what a worthless person you would be if you were to fail (iB), then you will tend to feel extreme anxiety and tension (C), which will interfere with your performance on the test to such an extent that you forget what you do know and, thereby, bring the feared event (failure) about.

On the other hand, if you have only rational beliefs (rB) about A, then, even though you may never like A, you will experience only a mild emotional response (C) that assists you to achieve what you want out of life. If you are about to take a test on which you may fail (A), and if you tell yourself that, even though failure would be unpleasant and disadvantageous, it certainly would not be the end of the world and you could still consider yourself a worthwhile human being (rB), you would then feel only mild anxiety (C) that would stimulate you to prepare well for the test, and thereby, increase the chance that you would pass it.

It is **not** the purpose of this book to suggest that you learn to like things or people you now dislike. Far from it. Indeed, you are encouraged to consider **likes, preferences,** and **wishes** to be perfectly normal and rational. It **is** one objective of this book to help you stop inflicting **needless** psychological pain on yourself: to help you change your **intense,** painful, debilitative feelings of hostility and depression to the **milder,** less painful, facilitative emotions of annoyance and displeasure; to help you deal with the unpleasant events of your life without being **unduly** upset in the process.

If you feel extremely upset at point C, then you very likely have some irrational beliefs at point B: and if you wish to change how you feel at point C, then you must change your beliefs at point B from irrational Beliefs (iB) to rational Beliefs (rB). Before you can do that, however, you may need to learn more about irrational beliefs. The next chapter will present some of the irrational beliefs commonly held in our society.

IV.   ELEVEN IRRATIONAL BELIEFS

Sociologists and anthropologists have demonstrated that all societies directly and indirectly teach their members to believe many senseless, irrational ideas. Chances are that many of your own beliefs are essentially irrational. Most of these beliefs you took over directly without even thinking about them, and you unthinkingly adopted them as your own without examining them or seeking evidence to support them.

Generally speaking, irrational beliefs are the assumptions upon which irrational self-talk is based. To take a silly example, suppose that you irrationally believe that you **need** carrots for supper in order to survive, and suppose also that you do not have any in the house. Very likely you would then engage in irrational self-talk like, "This is awful! I can't stand it! I should have remembered to get some! What a schmuck I am!!" On the other hand, if you more rationally believed that, while carrots would be nice, they were hardly necessary, then you might engage in more rational self-talk like, "It would be nice to have carrots for supper, and I wish I had some, but it is hardly catastrophic and I can stand it. Guess I'll just have corn instead."

Ellis (1962) has listed eleven irrational ideas that are prevalent in our society. Each of the beliefs is listed below, along with some of the reasons that each is irrational.

1. The idea that it is a dire necessity to be loved or approved by virtually every significant other person in his community (p. 61)

   While there is some evidence that children may need love; and while it is true that most of us **desire** the love and approval of others; there is no evidence to prove that adults **need** love and approval, either to feel happy or worthwhile. Indeed, many hermits seem to do quite well without it, and many others not so withdrawn seem to be happy getting their kicks out of **things** or **ideas**.

   Since there is no evidence that you **need** love and approval, your arbitrarily **defining** them as such is as silly as defining carrots as a need. If you define love and approval as a need, then any indication that some significant person does **not** love or approve of you will result in self-talk such as, "This is awful! I can't stand it! I must be a real shit! Poor me!" Such self-talk often leads to depression.

If you believe you **need** love and approval, then you will tend to behave in ingratiating, insecure, and ultimately annoying ways that will tend to lose you the very love and approval you so desperately demand. The slightest sign of disapproval will result in your becoming so upset that you cannot calmly, planfully go about regaining approval.

2. The idea that one should be thoroughly competent, adequate, and achieving in all possible respects if one is to consider oneself worthwhile (p. 63)

There is no evidence that people **need** success in order to feel happy or worthwhile. While there are **practical** advantages (such as money) to success in our society; and while it usually is more fun to win a tennis game, for example, than to lose it; it is quite possible to be happy though poor and it is also possible to enjoy tennis though losing, UNLESS you arbitrarily **define** success as a need.

If you believe that you **should** be successful in order to be worthwhile, usually you will do two irrational things: (1) you will rate yourself as worthless when you are not better than others, and (2) you will equate your worth as a person with the success of your performances. Both of these practices confuse your extrinsic with your intrinsic worth. You may make more or fewer mistakes than others, or than you yourself made in the past, but making mistakes has no implications for your worth as a person. You can never become more nor less than a fallible human being. And fallible humans make mistakes.

An **over** concern with achievement will result in your being so upset about the possibility of failure that you cannot do well at chosen tasks. If you **need** to do well on a test, and if you tell yourself that it would be "awful" to fail, then you will upset yourself to the extent that you will not be able to recall the information you know.

3. The idea that certain people are bad, wicked, or villainous and that they should be severely blamed and punished for their villainy

Recall Shakespeare's line, "There's nothing good or bad but thinking makes it so." There are no good or bad people in this world, only those who are considered to be bad by themselves or others. But defining people as bad doesn't any more make them bad than calling ghetto poor people rich would add any money to their bank accounts. There are only fallible humans who make errors.

When people behave in ways that are considered bad, they usually do so for one of three reasons: they are too unintelligent, or too ignorant, or too emotionally disturbed to refrain from doing so. In any of the three cases, they are neither bad nor do they deserve to be punished.

If no one deserves to be punished, then it is absurd to punish people because they deserve it. In many cases it may be sensible to **penalize** a person in the hope that he or someone else will not repeat the behavior we don't like in the future. But punishment just for the sake of punishment is irrational.

4. The idea that it is awful and catastrophic when things are not the way one would very much like them to be (p. 69)

   As Epictetus has said, "Men are disturbed not by things but the views they take of them" (today we might add "and so are women"). We must constantly remind ourselves that the source of values is human thought. So the President may be impeached, for example. "Wonderful!" say persons of the other political party. "That would be awful, terrible, and catastrophic," say many others. Now, obviously, impeachment of the President cannot be wonderful and catastrophic at the same time. Indeed, it is neither wonderful nor awful unless you subjectively define it as such.

   Reality is reality. There is no reason why you should like reality as it is, and it may be a good idea for you to strive very hard to change it. But the fact remains that if you constantly whine about reality and repeatedly tell yourself how awful and terrible things are, then you may upset yourself to the extent that you are less able to change the conditions you dislike.

5. The idea that human unhappiness is externally caused and that people have little or no ability to control their sorrows and disturbances (p. 72)

> The idea that unhappiness is externally caused is believed by almost everyone in our society, including most psychologists. When I say, "You make me so mad!," I directly imply that I can't feel happy (unmad) unless you change your behavior. If you are the cause of my unhappiness, then obviously I don't have to take any responsibility for my feelings. What a cop out! Ellis' theory of personality is truly revolutionary because it puts the responsibility for your feelings where it belongs—with you. It is a no-cop-out theory because it teaches that **you** are the one who determines how you feel.
>
> When I say, "You make me so mad!," I imply that you **ought** to change because of these awful feelings you are inflicting on .me. Wouldn't it be better (and more accurate) to say, "I am very angry at you right now! But I realize that I am creating my own anger by telling myself nonsense. Therefore, until I can get my head together, it might be best if we changed the topic (or stayed away from each other)"?
>
> When you say, "It hurts me" or "I can't stand it," you imply that "it" is controlling how you feel. "It" cannot affect you unless you arbitrarily **define** it as being awful and so terrible that you can't stand it.

6. The idea that if something is or may be dangerous or fearsome one should be terribly concerned about it and should keep dwelling on the possibility of its occurring (p. 75)

> A surprisingly large number of persons in our society have excessive fears and worries. And the list of things feared is almost endless: taking tests, speaking in public, riding in airplanes, expressing one's views to an administrative superior, being attacked by dogs or snakes, etc., etc.
>
> Excessive fears and worries usually do not prevent the feared event from occurring—indeed, excessive anxiety may **prevent** you from doing your best, and therefore, contribute to bringing the feared event about. Overconcern about failure in a test or

doing poorly in a speech interferes with performance to such an extent that you end up doing as poorly as you feared.

It makes good sense to do whatever is necessary to stave off the feared event, but when you ask yourself, "What's the **worst** that could possibly happen," an honest answer would be that you might fail at **this** particular task or that someone might consider you a fool. But failing at this task does not make you either a failure or a fool. The worst that can happen is never awful or terrible, it can never be more than unfortunate or inconvenient. You **can** stand it! Even dreaded events such as your death are nothing more than inevitable, natural occurrences— there is nothing terrible about them unless you believe them so.

7. The idea that it is easier to avoid than to face certain life difficulties and self-responsibilities (p. 78)

The thrust of this manual is to consider what **you** want out of life, but it should be emphasized that you are not likely to get it **via** short-term pleasure-seeking. Chances are that your own long-term self-interest will best be served by immersing yourself in some kind of work, or project, or cause, and by doing your best to create the kind of world in which you would like to live.

Your self-interest also demands an expression of social interest, mostly because you are unlikely to get what you want from life unless you cooperate with others. Another way of saying this is that selfishness is not in your long-term self-interest.

Living implies doing. Resting is often necessary and desirable, but as a steady diet it is deadly. Achievement-confidence almost always comes through mastery of various tasks, almost never through avoiding those that are difficult or unpleasant. Thus, after figuring out what **you** want from life, usually you will be best off to work hard to get it and uncomplainingly do what is necessary (no matter how much you dislike it), forcing yourself to get the unpleasant but necessary tasks out of the way as soon as possible.

Remember, however, that all work and no play

does make Jack a dull boy! Focusing exclusively on your long-term interests at the expense of necessary short-term recreation can also be deadly. You would be best off to avoid the extremes of rigid self-discipline and slothfulness.

8. The idea that one should be dependent on others and needs someone stronger than oneself on whom to rely (p. 80)

It would be senseless for you to refuse all help from others just to prove how strong you are, and it would be a good idea to seek help when you could really benefit from it. But the rational person realizes that he is essentially alone in this world and that he must make and be responsible for his own decisions.

Usually you would be best off to emphasize your tendencies toward individualism and independence because you are something that this world has never seen before—therefore, no one else really knows what you really feel nor what's best for you. You generally will be best off making your own decisions and depending on your own judgment. Even though it is in your self-interest to be cooperative, it almost never is best to be subservient to the wishes of others.

Ralph Waldo Emerson in his essay on *Self Reliance* said something that I believe to be appropriate here:

"There is a time in every man's education when he arrives at the conviction that envy is ignorance; that imitation is suicide; that he must take himself for better or worse as his portion; that though the wide universe is full of good, no kernel of nourishing corn can come to him but through his toil bestowed on that plot of ground which is given to him to till. The power which resides in him is new in nature, and none but he knows what that is which he can do, nor does he know until he has tried."

9. The idea that one's past history is an all-important determiner of one's present behavior and that because something once strongly affected one's life, it should indefinitely have a similar effect (p. 82)

Many modern psychologists teach that the past

determines the present—some even say that our personalities are formed by the time we are five years of age. This is obviously not true. While it cannot be denied that the past is important and that it **influences** how we behave today, and while it is true that self-change is difficult and work-requiring, it is possible to change. Just because in the past we have behaved in a particular way, we can learn to become different at any age.

It is not our past that determines our responses but our attitudes toward the past. Causes of present behavior exist only in the present. Even if you assume that the past influences the future, remember some common sayings: "Today is tomorrow's yesterday"; "Today is the first day of the rest of your life"; and "The present is the past of your future." "If you wish to be different tomorrow, make a small change today."

10. The idea that one should become quite upset over other people's problems and disturbances (p. 85)

When you feel upset about someone else who is disturbed, you feel upset not by **their** problems but by your irrational self-talk that they **shouldn't** behave that way. There is very little that you can do to change others, and upsetting yourself about their problems will not help at all. The best you can hope to do is to **try** to help them change in a **calm, objective** way, recognizing that you may fail but that you can stand it and make the best of a bad situation.

11. The idea that there is invariably a right, precise, and perfect solution to human problems and that it is catastrophic if this solution is not found (p. 87)

There is no perfection or certainty in the world, and to expect to find it is irrational. While searching for **feasible** solutions and personal improvements is a reasonable activity, compulsively searching for **the** perfect way to do something usually results in a decreased probability of finding a **practical** alternative. To err is human and to make less than completely adequate decisions is par for the course.

Do you believe any of Ellis' irrational ideas? Chances are good that you do, but there is no way to be certain because, as

Ellis (1969) points out, many of your irrational beliefs are:

> "... At least in part, unconscious rather than conscious. The individual often consciously knows that it is silly to expect everyone to love him, to hope to do perfectly all the time, to be able to stand any frustration, or to worry about threatening possibilities. But, unconsciously, he firmly and deeply believes this nonsense; and, again unconsciously, he keeps telling himself over and over that he **should** be loved, **must** do well, **should not** be frustrated, should worry over possible accidents, and the like. His conscious views, therefore, are seriously in conflict with his unconscious values ..." (p. 63)

Whether or not your irrational beliefs are conscious, they are a basic cause of your present intense, sustained emotions. If you believe the kind of nonsense suggested by these eleven irrational ideas, it is likely that you will feel at least to some extent fearful, hostile, depressed, or guilty. If you could change your beliefs to rational ideas, it would be difficult to experience any of these feelings in intense form, at least not for any great length of time.

But before you can change your own beliefs, you will need to find out what they are. The next chapter will present some techniques that are designed to help you identify some irrational ideas that you may believe.

V. IDENTIFY YOUR IRRATIONAL BELIEFS

How can you learn to identify your irrational beliefs? In helping students and counselees learn how to do this, I have found the ABC approach to be a helpful teaching technique (remember, A is the **Activating Event**; B is your **Belief** about the activating event; and C is the emotional **Consequence**). Here is how to do it:

Step number 1

Monitor your emotional reactions. Whenever you experience an unpleasant, debilitative emotion (C), describe it as accurately as you can. Say, "I feel **(for example, angry)**." Below are some words that you may wish to use. "I feel _____":

angry	hateful
ashamed	hurt
bored	jealous
depressed	mad
discouraged	oppressed
disgusted	resentful
exploited	scared
frightened	sorrowful
grief-stricken	unhappy
guilty	upset
	worried

Sometimes you will experience two or more negative emotions at the same time. For example, you might say, "I feel **angry** at Joe, and I feel **guilty** because I yelled and screamed at him." Write down all the unpleasant feelings that you experience at a particular time. Let it all hang out.

Step number 2

Describe the Activating Event. Write down your perception of the event, or thing, that seemed to "trigger" the chain of events that led to C (the emotional Consequence). Here are some common types of activating events:

Something that someone else said, did, or thought

Something that someone else might say, do, or think if you do what you want to do

Some general social condition, such as racism, sexism, crime, poverty, injustice, etc.

Something you have done in the past that you consider to be immoral, illegal, or just plain stupid

Something that is coming up at which you may fail or otherwise perform poorly, or which may be dangerous

Some thoughts or feelings you have or have had

etc.

Here is an example of steps 1 and 2 completed by Mrs. G., a teacher with whom I worked:

1. **C (Emotional Consequence):** I often feel anger at Jimmy and disgust at myself. Sometimes I feel so discouraged that I think about giving up teaching.

2. **A (Activating Event):** Jimmy interrupts me every time I start speaking to the class. He often makes jeering remarks to me and the other students, and he hums or sings aloud whenever he feels like it. He opens and closes his books with a bang—I guess noise distraction is his specialty. His school work, when done, is sloppy and incomplete, and his handwriting is illegible.

Step number 3

As accurately as you can, **record your self-talk at point B**. The first few times you do this, you may find it difficult, if not impossible, to complete this step. Over the years particular pairs of Activating events (A) and emotional Consequences (C) may have occurred so frequently that C seems "automatically" to follow A. After years of being criticized by your mother at point A, you may not be aware of what you are saying to yourself at point B in order to cause your feelings of anger at point C. What you say to yourself has become "unconscious," not necessarily in the Freudian sense, but in the sense of being out of current awareness.

The process may be analogous to what occurs when you learn to drive a car. At first your self-talk about starting the car, putting it in gear, accelerating, and braking are all quite apparent. After driving many years, however, your driving behaviors become so habitual that you may not be aware of any self-talk. Similarly, in a frequently occurring emotional experience, what you say to yourself at point B may become a sort of emotional "shorthand" such that your self-talk is compressed into a very short period of time (Maultsby, 1971).

My experience with teaching this approach has convinced

me that, even though it may be **difficult** for many people to become aware of their self-talk, most people **can** learn to do so. Chances are that you can, too, with a little effort. Here's how.

After you have described A and C, ask yourself, "What **must** I have been saying to myself about A at point B in order to experience the emotion I did at point C?" Going back to the case of Mrs. G., what **must** she have been saying to herself in order to feel anger at Jimmy and disgust at herself?

Obviously, she was **not** saying to herself, "Hey this is great! Jimmy's finally showing some assertiveness! I must be a pretty great teacher to help him feel comfortable enough to express himself like this!" If this had been her self-talk, then she probably would have felt elation and self-pride. She probably was saying something else to herself, perhaps along the following lines:

(1) I don't like the way Jimmy is behaving!
(2) He shouldn't do that!
(3) His constant disturbing behavior is awful! I can't stand it!
(4) I **should** be able to handle bad kids like him!
(5) I guess I'll **never** be a good teacher!

Some of your self-talk may be perfectly rational. For example, Mrs. G.'s saying that "I don't like the way Jimmy is behaving!" is rational because there is no reason why you shouldn't dislike anything you obviously do. There is nothing irrational about any of your likes, dislikes, wishes, and preferences.

On the other hand, if your self-talk sentences indicate a belief in one of the eleven ideas discussed in the last chapter, assume that they are irrational. Another simple indicator of the probable irrationality of any self-talk is the use of: (1) highly **evaluative** words like **should, ought,** or **must**; (2) catastrophizing words like, "It's awful!"; "It's terrible!"; or "I can't stand it!"; or (3) overgeneralizations, such as "I **can't** do that!," or "I'll **never** find another girl like her," or "I'm really a **rotten person!**" Going back to Mrs. G.'s self-talk, notice that she says that Jimmy **should** be different (sentence number 2) and that **she should** be different (sentence number 4); she used **catastrophizing** words (sentence number 3); and she **overgeneralized** (sentence number 5). All of her irrational self-verbalizations are a matter of opinion: there is no **evidence** to support them. While it would be nice if she and Jimmy were perfect, and it may be true that she made some mistake with Jimmy in the past, there is no reason why either she or Jimmy **should** be different from what they are. And while Jimmy's behavior may be inconvenient, it is not awful or terrible. And just because she has had difficulty with some aspects of her teaching in the past is no reason to conclude that she will **never** improve.

Summary

Your own strong, negative emotions are **signals** that "something is wrong." Usually that "something" is some irrational nonsense that you believe. If you wish to identify what it is that you are saying to yourself when you feel upset: (1) describe as accurately as you can how you feel, (2) describe the activating event that seemed to "trigger" the feelings, and (3) record your self-talk—what you can recall saying to yourself or what you must have been saying to yourself at point B. Look especially for highly evaluative, judgmental, demanding sentences; for catastrophizing, whining sentences; and for over-generalizations.

The next chapter will attempt to show more specifically why each of these types of self-verbalization is irrational, and it will also present some more rational alternatives.

VI. DISPUTE YOUR IRRATIONAL BELIEFS

If you wish to change the irrational beliefs and self-verbalizations that you discover at point B, then it would be a good idea to go on to the next step, D, to **Dispute** the nonsense you are telling yourself. Since, as has been said, almost all irrational self-verbalizations include the evaluative words "should" and "ought"; or the catastrophizing words "It's awful!," "It's terrible!," and "I can't stand it!"; or overgeneralizations such as "I will never be able to do it," and "I am a bad person"; these types of sentences will be analyzed in detail.

Shoulds and Oughts

Very few of us believe that events come about by magic; that is, most of us accept the idea that natural events have natural causes. If you accept the idea that events are caused, then you must agree that it doesn't make sense to assert that things **should** be different from what they are. If you see a stone falling toward the ground, for example, it would be absurd to say that the stone **should** be falling sideways. Similarly, if your friend is emotionally disturbed, there isn't any reason why she **should** behave calmly and rationally.

Now it may be true that it would be **nice** if the stone fell sideways or if your friend behaved calmly, and it may be that it would be a **good idea** to work very hard to help your friend behave rationally, but there isn't any reason that an emotionally disturbed person (or anyone else) **should** behave differently than she obviously does, and there is every reason of heredity and environmental experience for her to behave exactly as she does!

What's the point? The point is that we often upset ourselves by **demanding** that we, or other people, or reality in general **should** be different than it is, and if we or the world aren't exactly as we think they **should** be, that's pretty awful!

So Suzie calls you a name at point A and you get angry at point C. You couldn't become angry if you weren't saying to yourself something like "She **shouldn't** do that!"

Why **shouldn't** she call you names? True, it would be **nicer** if she didn't call you names, and it would be more **pleasant** if she said nice things instead. It makes perfectly good sense for you to prefer that Suzie behave differently or to **wish** that Suzie were an angel, but to **demand** that Suzie **should** be different is absurd, because considering Suzie's heredity and history and her past relationships with you or others like you, there is every reason for her to behave **exactly** as she does and no reason whatsoever for her to behave according to your preferences.

Each of us has to some extent a Jehovah complex which manifests itself as a **demand** that we and the rest of the world be as we would prefer them to be. But we are not Jehovah, obviously. Therefore, our demands are irrational.

Now don't get me wrong. There isn't any reason why you shouldn't demand anything you want to! Given the culture you were brought up in, you probably acquired many shoulds and oughts and musts, and, therefore, there is every reason why you, too, should behave exactly as you do. You would **be better off**, however, if you would give up your essentially irrational demands that the world be different, and, instead, accept the idea that the world is pretty much as it is, that what exists has natural causes, and that it is not likely to change very much for the better unless all of us calmly, rationally, and cooperatively work very hard to change it.

A very high percentage of irrational self-talk contains the words should or should not. Not all uses of the word should are irrational, however. Vertes (1971) has pointed out that there are two uses of the word should: (1) the should of probability, and (2) the should of obligation.

The should of probability is quite rational, and its use in this way is unlikely to lead to negative emotions. This usage occurs when you say things like "There should be snow in the mountains in January" or "If I press the alarm button on the clock it should stop ringing," or "Since the plane is due at 10:00 P.M. and it is now 9:45 P.M., it should be here in a few minutes." All of these are merely different ways of saying that there is a high probability that certain events will take place. All very rational.

The second use of the word should, however, is quite irrational, and therefore, quite likely to lead to unpleasant emotions. When I say, "I believe that people should be on time for meetings," if I am using the should of obligation I am **not** saying that it is highly probable that they will be at meetings on time. Rather I am saying that they **ought** to be at meetings on time and that they are to be blamed and criticized when they are not. When I say, "I should do better than that!," usually I'm saying that I **ought** to behave better and, unless I do, I'm not a very worthwhile person.

There seems to me to be a third use of the word should. For example, when I say, "Kids should get a lot of exercise and sunshine," usually I mean that it would be **a good idea** if kids got these things. This use also seems to me to be quite rational.

It is a good idea to look out for the shoulds of obligation when analyzing your self-talk in order to identify irrationality. Sometimes it is difficult to find them because you may disguise your shoulds by asking rhetorical questions such as "How can she do this to me?" or "Why is she doing this to me?" When you ask questions like this, usually you are not really seeking answers. You are asserting, in disguised form, that "She **should not** do this to me!"

There may be no doubt that you would **prefer** that she not do this to you, and it may make perfectly good sense to **wish** that she behaved differently, and it may be sensible to try to **change** her behavior toward you, but to **demand** that she **should** behave differently is to want to be God and say that "Everything **should** be as I prefer it to be!" But that's nonsense! Why should anyone or anything behave according to your preferences merely because you demand it?

Most major religious leaders have stressed the advantages to ourselves and others in becoming less highly evaluative, less judgmental. For example, Jesus is reported to have said, "Judge not that ye be not judged," and "Let him who is perfect cast the first stone." One basic message of this teaching, it seems to me, is that if you have very strong opinions about what other persons **should** be like and what you **ought** to be doing, if you **demand** that they and you and the world **should** be different, then you are doomed to personal unhappiness. Because neither you nor the world will ever meet your unrealistic expectations, your use of these shoulds of obligation is irrational, and you would be better off to drop them from your vocabulary.

Dispute your shoulds. When you discover yourself using the should of obligation, ask yourself: **why** should X (the world in general, other people, you, etc.) be different from what it undoubtedly is? Where is the **evidence** that X should be different? "Where is it writ that X ought to be as I very much would like it to be?" The answer to these questions, of course, is that there is no reason why things should be different; there is no evidence; and there is no place that it is writ. Say to yourself: "I don't like X; I wish to hell that X did not exist or that X were different; it surely would be nice if I could change X, and I'll try to do it, but if I fail, I can stand it," or "It doesn't seem that there's much I can do about it right now. Tough shit." If you can say these rational sentences to yourself and learn to believe them, you still will not like X, you still may feel irritated or annoyed that X exists, but you will not inflict the needless pain of extreme anger or depression on yourself.

Awfuls and Terribles

A second type of self-talk that leads to unnecessary negative emotions is catastrophizing. It is not unusual to hear persons complain about something's being "awful" or "terrible," or to complain that they "just can't stand it!" The basic reason that catastrophizing is irrational is that there is no objective evidence for the terms used. That is, it is impossible to prove that **anything** or **anybody** is awful or terrible or that you can't stand it. There is **nothing** in the universe that is awful or terrible, unless you arbitrarily define it so, and there is very little that you can't stand. If you truly can't stand something, for example, extreme physical pain, chances are you will lose consciousness and will no longer experience it.

Now this is not to say that things or people couldn't be improved! And there is no doubt that some events are inconvenient and unfortunate. That much we may be able to prove. But you cannot prove that something is awful.

So your sweetheart leaves you, for example. Now it may be true that such an event would be unfortunate because you would not have her doing nice things for you, and it might be inconvenient because it might take some time to find a new girl friend. But it would not be awful, and you would be able to stand it. Losing your sweetheart is never fatal unless you convince yourself that it is so terrible that you can't stand it and that you may as well end it all.

Irrational catastrophizing almost inevitably leads to unpleasant emotions. Whenever you whine over and over about how awful something is, you eventually believe yourself and become quite angry and/or depressed. You would do much better if you stopped your senseless whining and dropped such language from your vocabulary.

Usually, evaluative and catastrophizing statements are used together, either explicitly or implicitly. "**I should** be different," and "The world generally **should** be different from what it is"; and "It's **awful** and **terrible** that things are not different"; and "**I just can't stand things**, including me, the way they are now!" If you have nonsense like this running around in your head, you are bound to feel angry or depressed or both.

Dispute your catastrophizing. When you hear yourself say the words "awful" or "terrible" or "I can't stand it," ask yourself, "**Why** is X awful? Where is the **evidence** that X is terrible? **Is it really true** that I can't stand it? I can prove that I don't like X, or that I feel uncomfortable or annoyed in the presence of X, or that X can make life more difficult for me, but the fact that I don't like X or am inconvenienced by it doesn't prove that X is awful or terrible! Besides, I **can** stand it. If I truly couldn't stand it, I would die or pass out. The fact that I am neither dead nor unconscious proves that I can stand it. Now it may be wise to say 'I **won't** stand **for** it!' and to try to change X, but even if X remains exactly as it is, though I may never learn to like it, I can stand it!"

Overgeneralizations

"All Indians walk in single file: at least the one I saw was." Some of the generalizations we draw about our experiences are as absurd as this one.

When a loved one rejects us, we tend to say, "I'll **never** find another girl like her," or "That proves that I'm an unlovable person." Actually, if we try, we may find someone we will like even more than the one who left us—never is a long time! And because one person doesn't love us doesn't prove that no one **ever** will.

Similarly, when you say, "I **can't** do X," all you can really say rationally is that " **up to now**, I have failed when attempting X, but, who knows, maybe next time or next year I will be able to do it if I keep trying."

Another common overgeneralization is to equate our self-worth with our performances or characteristics: when we fail at something we say, "I'm a failure," and when someone does something we do not approve of, we say, "He's a bad person." Suppose, however, that you have one hundred performances in your repertoire, including reading, walking, singing, making love, being kind to others, etc., which are considered by you or others to be neutral or good acts; but one of your hundred acts is considered bad—you beat someone else over the head, for example. Now you have ninety-nine acts that are considered good and one that is considered bad. Are you a good person or a bad person? Obviously, you are neither, because you cannot meaningfully generalize from your acts to your worth or value as a human being. Similarly, failing at one or a few things does not make you a failure.

Dispute your overgeneralizations. Ask yourself, "Where's the evidence that I'm a failure just because I made a mistake? How can I prove that I'll **never** get or find X? Is it really true that I can't do X, or isn't it more consistent with the facts that **up to now** I have failed at X, but I may succeed next time? Now it's true that I'm a fallible human who is bound to make mistakes. I'll try to improve my **performances** in the future, but even if I fail again, I'm still nothing more nor less than a fallible human. When I do something that I or someone else considers a mistake, I sometimes say, 'Here I am, over forty years old and still making mistakes! Maybe I'll be perfect when I'm fifty.' " That's usually good for a laugh.

Summary

When you feel a negative, debilitative emotion at C, chances are that you are saying to yourself at B some variation of one of the self-verbalizations described above. When you do find irrational self-verbalizations such as these, dispute them (D) by asking questions such as: "Where's the evidence or proof? Why is this so? How can it be? etc." When you have convinced yourself that there is no evidence to prove your irrational self-talk, substitute more rational self-talk that would result in milder, more facilitative feelings. More about that in the next chapter.

VII. RATIONAL–EMOTIVE HOMEWORK

In this chapter we will try to integrate what was presented in the last few chapters. The format for this integration is called Rational-Emotive Homework (REH).

REH is an assignment that routinely is given clients when they are receiving rational-emotive therapy. I have used it as an assignment in classes I teach as well. Because it personalizes the principles being taught, REH seems to be a very effective method of teaching the principles of rational living and of letting the counselor or teacher know whether his or her client or students have learned the material.

When you do REH, you will follow three simple (?) steps:

1. **Describe the Activating Event (A) and the emotional Consequence (C).**
2. **Record your self-talk (B).** Write down and number, sentence-by-sentence, what you said to yourself at point B. If you initially are unable to recall what you said, write down what you probably were saying to yourself about A in order to feel emotionally upset at C.
3. **Dispute your irrational beliefs (D).** Go back to the sentences you wrote down in step 2 and do three things: a. categorize each sentence according to whether it indicates a rational Belief (rB) or an irrational Belief (iB); b. explain **why** the belief is rational or irrational; and c. write some alternative rational self-talk that you could use in the future to keep from needlessly upsetting yourself.

Some people ask, "Do I have to write all this down? Can't I just do it in my head?" My response is that there isn't any reason why you **should** do anything, but that other people have found that it helped them to become more fully aware of what they were doing when they write it out on paper.

Let's go back to Mrs. G., the teacher who was upset about Jimmy's behavior in the classroom, and see how her problem fits the Rational-Emotive Homework format:

C (**Emotional Consequence**): I often feel anger at Jimmy and disgust at myself. Sometimes I feel so discouraged that I think about giving up teaching.

A (**Activating Event**): Jimmy interrupts me every time I start speaking to the class. He often makes jeering remarks to me and the other students, and he hums or sings aloud whenever he feels like it. He opens and closes his books with a bang–I guess noise distraction is his specialty. His school work, when done, is sloppy and incomplete, and his handwriting is illegible.

B (Beliefs and Self-Verbalizations): (1) I don't like the way Jimmy is behaving! (2) He shouldn't do that! (3) His constant disturbing behavior is awful! I can't stand it! (4) I **should** be able to handle bad kids like him! (5) I guess I'll **never** be a good teacher!

D (Dispute): (The numbered comments under D refer back to the numbered self-verbalizations under B.)

1. rB. This sentence is rational because there isn't any reason why I should like the way Jimmy is behaving. It is perfectly rational to like or prefer anything I obviously do.

2. iB. This sentence indicates an irrational belief in the idea that people **shouldn't** do the things they do. This is irrational because, given Jimmy's heredity, his history, and his environment, there is every reason that he **should** behave exactly as he does. It would be **nice** if he would change, and I **wish** he would, but there really isn't any reason he **should** behave differently merely because I demand it. After all! Only God can have everything She demands! Jimmy appears to be a disturbed child–is it reasonable to expect a disturbed child to act like a model student?

3. iB. This sentence indicates an irrational belief in the idea that I can't stand it when things aren't as I would like them to be. This is irrational because there is no evidence that I can't stand it. I have stood it up to now, and if I stop indoctrinating myself with how **awful** and **terrible** it is, that is, if I stop whining, I will be able to stand it easily. I don't expect that I'll ever learn to like Jimmy's behavior, but I can remind myself that, at worst, it's too bad or it's inconvenient, but it's never terrible, never awful.

4. iB. This sentence indicates a belief in the irrational idea that I need to do well in order to consider myself worthwhile. My self-talk is irrational because there is no reason that I **should** be able to do anything perfectly well. After all, I'm a fallible human being who can be expected to make mistakes. Okay, maybe I have made

some mistakes in my interactions with Jimmy in the past, but even if I did make mistakes, there isn't any reason that I shouldn't have made them. Given my characteristics as a person and the training I've had, there is every reason to expect me to behave as I do, too. True, it would be **nice** to be able to handle kids like him, but it's not **necessary** to be able to do so in order to consider myself a worthwhile person.

I notice that I called Jimmy a "bad" kid. This is another irrational idea. There is no such thing as a bad kid, only kids whose behaviors I don't happen to like. And just because I don't happen to like Jimmy's behavior doesn't mean that he **deserves** to be punished. Maybe I can try **penalizing** some of his behavior, but if that doesn't change it, maybe I'll try something else, like reinforcing the behaviors I like and ignoring those I don't like.

5. iB.   This sentence is irrational because I am overgeneralizing. Even though I do **some** things less than perfectly, and even though I have had **difficulty** doing some things **in the past** this doesn't prove either that I'm a poor teacher or that I can't improve my teaching performance in the future! Even if I never improve my performance as a teacher, however, I can still accept myself as a person, a fallible human being, who deserves to be as happy as she can be just because she's alive.

Following are two more examples of assignments done by students in my counseling classes. They have been modified to some extent to conceal the identity of the students involved and to make them consistent with the ABCD format.

REH Example Number One

A.   **Activating Event**
The kids in an organization I was working with were going on a trip in two buses. As the coordinator of the program, I was supervisor for one of the buses. About five miles south of town the bus started making a frightful buzzing sound. The bus driver yelled angrily that someone was pushing a fire door. We checked and no one was, but she kept looking angrily over her shoulder, telling us to be quiet and sit down. I moved forward and asked if I could help. Yes, she snapped, you can SIT DOWN, and TAKE

THAT SIGN OFF THE BACK WINDOW and BE QUIET and MAKE EVERYONE ELSE BE QUIET! My mouth dropped open and with fire shooting out of my head, I sat down with a grim, steamy look on my face.

B.   **Beliefs and Self-Talk About A**
   1. She can't get away with that!
   2. Especially with me; she shouldn't treat me like that.
   3. Everyone is looking at me and no matter what I do I'll look dumb.
   4. It's not fair, all I wanted to do was help.
   5. I'm an innocent victim, poor me.
   6. She shouldn't act like that.
   7. She's setting a bad example for the volunteers and kids. How terrible!
   8. She is really a bitch.
   9. They shouldn't have sent such an awful person. The two people last year were wonderful but this year they had to get a power-drunk neurotic. How terrible!
   10. But worse, I can't think of a single thing to do that would be mean enough to pay her back or forceful enough to show her I'm boss, not her. How frustrating, how dreadful, how outrageously UNFAIR!

C.   **Consequences of Beliefs and Self-Talk**
   I was furious and embarrassed.

D.   **Dispute Your Beliefs and Self-Talk**
   I think that all my self-talk in the B section was irrational. What follows is what I consider more rational self-talk.

   1. Why yes, she can get away with it. She did, didn't she?
   2. Say, Miss Conceited, why pick yourself out for special privileges; it would be nice if she didn't treat anyone like that, but you're not God, nor have you received special dispensation for universal respect. Shoot, look on the bright side, at least she's democratic, she's nasty to everyone!
   3. That's probably not true, actually. Hardly anyone is looking at me, and those who are, are doubtless in total sympathy with me. Even if they do think I'm

dumb, however, that hardly makes me a dumb person.

4. Sure it's not fair by my standards. But what do I expect from life; everyone doing what I think they should do all the time? If she doesn't want my help, that's her right. I offered it but I can't force it on anyone.

5. She didn't **make** me angry, I did, so I'm not an innocent victim of a cruel world. When I stop being angry, I won't be "poor me" any more.

6. Hey, toots, you're not God who legislates "shoulds." It would be a helluva lot nicer for everyone if she **didn't** act that way, but if she does, she does.

7. The volunteers and kids have had a lot more experience with irrational people than I have lately. They're doing fine and don't need my protection. If one person can upset what they've learned, then it wasn't much of an education. It's unfortunate that this happened, but it's not terrible.

8. Name calling, and I'll just get madder. Actually, she's **not** a bitch. She's acting upset, rude, irrational, angry, inconsiderate of others' feelings, but she's really **not** a female dog. And even if she were a bitch, what do I expect a bitch to be, an angel?

9. There I go again, shouldn'ting. They **did** send her and maybe I can do something to prevent that next time, but let's live with her for now the best we can. Tut, tut, name calling again!

10. If I "paid her back," I'd be even madder at myself. Besides, think of how much time and energy I'd save if I didn't addle my brain about a punishment. I can't expect **her** to be rational, but I can expect me to be.

NEXT TIME I COULD THINK

Woops, she's really upset! Did I do anything to help her upset herself? No, I don't think so though I may have been moving around a lot more than she would have liked. Did anyone else do anything to warrant this response? No, they all checked to see if the emergency doors were closed and they weren't, so we've done what we could. It's unfortunate that she's upset and acting so hatefully to everyone, but we'll survive and it will only make it worse for everyone if I feel or act hateful back.

Let's see, we'll move the sign, and I'll sit down and ask everyone to please be quiet for a bit until we find out what's going on. Then we'll wait to let her work things out and if I have any concerns about the future moves I'll voice them later when she has calmed down. And even later, I'll ask that she not go with us on any more trips.

REH Example Number Two

A. **Activating Event**
   Freddy called me a bastard.

B. **Beliefs and Self-Talk About A**
   1. How could he do that to me!
   2. Why does he do these terrible things!
   3. He deserves to be punished!
   4. He probably doesn't like me very much and that really hurts.

C. **Consequences of Beliefs and Self-Talk**
   Anger and depression.

D. **Dispute Your Beliefs and Self-Talk**
   1. iB. A direct answer would be "EASILY," since it doesn't take much effort to call someone names. Actually, my question probably was rhetorical in that I wasn't seeking an answer. What I really meant was that he **shouldn't** have called me a bastard! Actually, there are very good reasons for people behaving the way they do, including low intelligence, ignorance, and emotional disturbance. In Freddy's case, considering his home life, it is not surprising that he uses language like that; and considering that he appeared quite angry it's not surprising that he called me a name. It would have been nice if he had not been angry, and it would have been more pleasant if he had not called me a bastard, but there is no reason why he **should** behave as I expect him to.

   2. iB. The most direct answer would be that he probably learned to do these things. However, again, this appears to be a rhetorical question. What I really mean is that he **shouldn't** behave in this way. Why **should** he behave as I demand that he behave? It may make sense to try to change his behavior, and I may

have a "right" to expect him to behave differently, but if I do have these strong expectations of others, I inevitably will upset myself because inevitably, others will not behave according to my Jehovah-like demands.

3.   iB.   Actually, there is no reason that anyone deserves to be punished. Even if I believe that Freddy made a mistake in calling me a bastard, why shouldn't he, as a fallible human being, be expected to make lots of mistakes? Freddy is not a bad person, he's only a person who has some behaviors that I happen not to like. Perhaps if I work at it, I can get him to change those behaviors. In the meantime, both he and I would be better off if I accepted him as he is—a fallible human being.

4.   iB.   Assuming that Freddy doesn't like me much, how can that possibly hurt me? When someone calls me a bastard, there are only two possibilities: one, he is right, and I might thank him for bringing this to my attention so that I can stop being a bastard (from his point of view) in the future; two, he is wrong, he has made an error in perception. In either case, why must I upset myself? I wish Freddy would not call me a bastard and I would much prefer that he like me because he would then be less likely to harm me physically and more likely to help me get what I want out of life. In the future, I will behave differently and maybe he'll like me better. But, if he doesn't that's tough. I can stand it. After all, there is no way he can control my feelings!

A large percentage of persons who have completed REH have reported personal benefits to them, generally in the form of greater acceptance of self and others and in decreased incidence and degree of emotional upset. I sincerely hope that you are able to get the same benefits.

Some people have found it easier to do their REH assignments when using a form such as that found on the next page. If you wish to do your first few assignments on a form such as this, you will find some you may use in Appendix A of this book.

RATIONAL–EMOTIVE HOMEWORK FORM

When filling out this form, please write legibly. It will be easiest to complete the form correctly if you respond to the sections in this order: C first, then A, then B, and D last.

A. **ACTIVATING EVENT.** Describe your perceptions of the events that "triggered" your emotional upset, e.g., taking a test; your boyfriend telling you he's leaving you for another girl; an acquaintance insulting you, etc.

B. **BELIEFS and Self-Talk About A.** Record what you said to yourself, or what you **must** have said to yourself about the event. Please number each sentence. Examples: 1. **He shouldn't have done that!** 2. **It's awful and I can't stand it!** 3. **He's a very bad person for having done that!**

C. **CONSEQUENCES** of Your Beliefs and Self-Talk. Describe **feelings**, e.g., **anger, fear, depression, guilt**.

D. **DISPUTE Your Beliefs and Self-Talk.** For each sentence in your B section: decide if it is rational (rB) or irrational (iB); explain why it is rational or irrational; and write alternative rational self-talk.

VIII.   APPLYING RATIONAL–EMOTIVE PRINCIPLES

This chapter presents some additional techniques that are based on rational-emotive theory. They attempt to help you move gradually toward real-life applications of the ABCD material that you (hopefully) have been learning.

As stated in the last chapter, if you have emotional problems, one way to solve them is by means of an ABCD Rational-Emotive Homework (REH) approach. You will need to discover the irrational beliefs (iB) that you have about the activating event (A) and that are causing you unpleasant emotional consequences (C). You will then need to dispute (D) those beliefs and change them to more rational alternative beliefs (rB).

After you have completed an ABCD analysis, you may wish to engage in Rational-Emotive Imagery (REI), in which you calmly **imagine** being in a situation, behaving and feeling as you hope to behave and feel in the future. If you can successfully complete REH and REI, you probably will be significantly less emotionally upset and upsetable than you are now.

Rational-Emotive Imagery (REI)

Dr. Maxie Maultsby (1971) has developed a technique to be used after you have learned to do ABCD Rational-Emotive Homework but before you try new behaviors—in a real-life situation. Here is how he suggests you do it:

> For at least a half hour per day (longer if possible) you are to recreate, in your mind, the details of some event which you analyzed in the ABCD format. You are to actually see yourself in the same situation with everything exactly the way it was and everyone except you behaving as they actually did. You are to picture yourself behaving and feeling as you hope to behave and feel after you develop RSM (Rational Self-Mastery). So, for self-talk you shall use only "D" section material . . . Until you have learned to do ABC analyses sufficiently well . . . it is best not to begin REI (p. 63).

> For maximum benefit from REI, it is essential to remain calm while doing it. If you start to become upset, discontinue the imagery and re-read your

> homework. If you are still convinced that the "D" section contains no errors in rational thinking . . . you should try REI again the following day. If you become upset during the second attempt, you should discontinue further REI until that homework has been checked by your counselor (p. 64).

There is considerable recent psychological research demonstrating that, if you are able to **imagine** being **calm** in a situation, you will likely be able to **be** calm in the real situation. If you are seeing a counselor at present, she (or he) may be able to teach you how to relax very deeply, which will facilitate your doing REI effectively.

Up to this point in the book the emphasis has been on what goes on inside your head—your **perceptions** of an activating event at A, your **thoughts** about A at point B, the **emotional** consequence of your thinking at point C, your **dispute** of irrational beliefs at D, and your **imagination** of appropriate feelings and actions in rational-emotive imagery.

The next few techniques emphasize to a greater extent · your overt **actions**, especially as they relate to your thoughts and emotions.

Rational-Emotive Activity Homework

The most straightforward extension of Rational-Emotive Homework (REH), described in the last chapter, is what might be termed Activity Homework. After you have completed a successful REH homework project and you have been able to engage in **calm** Rational-Emotive Imagery (REI), the logical next step for you is to try your skills in real-life settings.

For example, if in the past you have been extremely anxious when meeting new people, **force** yourself to meet three new people this week. If you have difficulty with getting angry whenever you talk to your bigoted mother-in-law, **force** yourself to visit her this week instead of avoiding her.

The primary purpose of Activity Homework is, first, to give you an opportunity to observe and become more aware of self-talk while you actually are in a situation in which you typically get upset; second, to dispute your self-talk while there, and third, to discover that if you can learn to engage in rational self-talk in that situation, you will then be much more calm and relaxed while there. You will find that it is not **terrible** to talk to new people as long as you do not define it as such; you will find that it is **not** your mother-in-law who is making you angry, but rather **you** who are making you angry by **demanding** that she meet your expectations. Who knows? You may even learn to like meeting new people and your mother-in-law when you no longer make yourself so afraid and/or angry! Whether or not you learn to like certain kinds of situations, repeated successful experience in them will help you avoid **needlessly** upsetting yourself in them.

Rational Emotional Expression

One of my counseling clients reported that doing rational-emotive homework had enabled her to deal satisfactorily with some long-standing emotional problems that she had been having with her family, especially her sister, but that she had experienced some difficulty during the previous weekend when she went to visit a friend and his wife. She reported that from the moment she entered their house she was quite ill at ease. She asked me what she could have done about that.

My response was that "When you experience any unpleasant emotion at point C, immediately ask yourself, 'What am I saying to myself to create these feelings at point B? What kind of bull am I telling myself?' When you discover what you are saying to yourself, dispute it and start telling yourself rational sentences!" Her reply to that was, "You must have to be a tremendously fast thinker in order to use the ABCD approach and maintain a social conversation at the same time!"

She was correct in her suggestion that it may be difficult, especially for those new to it, to use the ABCD system in an unanticipated situation. If you have done a REH project and have engaged in REI, very likely you directed your attention to something that occurred in the past that still bothered you or to something that was sure to come up in the future, such as giving a speech, taking a test, or periodically interacting with your wife about whose responsibility it is to "discipline" the children. In an unanticipated situation, however, it is unlikely that you will "have your game together" to the point that you can rapidly deal rationally with it. What can you do?

One solution to the problem of a strong, negative feeling that you cannot control through rational thinking is to **express** the feeling. I told my client that when she felt ill at ease she could have said something like, "I'm feeling very uncomfortable right now!" When expressing feelings it is important for you to know, however, that expression of feelings can be either constructive or destructive of close interpersonal relationships, depending on whether it is done in a rational or irrational way.

The basic criteria by which to judge whether or not your expressions of feeling are rational are: (1) the degree to which they are statements of fact, and (2) the degree to which they suggest that you take responsibility for how you feel. "You are making me feel very uncomfortable!" states that others are responsible for your feelings of discomfort, which is not a fact because only you can make yourself uncomfortable by telling yourself irrational nonsense; and it implies that others **ought to change** what they are doing because they are inflicting these awful feelings on you, which is socially manipulative and non-accepting of personal responsibility.

If you recognize yourself as the cause of your feelings, it is rational, non-manipulative, and constructive to say, "I am feeling uncomfortable," or "I am very angry at you!" You might then add (**not** in these words), "But I realize that I am creating my own feelings of discomfort or anger through the bullshit I'm telling myself. I am not suggesting that you change your behavior because of how I feel, but it may be to our mutual advantage if we change the topic of discussion or if we leave the area and meet again at a later time when I have my head together. If we don't, because of my present emotional problem, I may do or say something that one or both of us may later regret."

Rational expression of feeling takes the basic form of what has been termed "feeling description" by some social psychologists and "I messages" by others. Both of these approaches to expression of feeling begin with "I feel," followed by the name of an emotion, e.g., "angry," "hostile," "depressed," "anxious," "fearful," etc.

Irrational expression of feelings, on the other hand, can take many forms:

a.   **"You messages"**: "You make me so mad!" "You really frighten me!"
b.   **Labeling**: "Jim is really crude." "You are self-centered."
c.   **Commands**: "Shut up." "Get out of here!"
d.   **Name Calling**: "He's a male chauvinist pig." "You're a creep."
e.   **Sarcasm**: "You really know how to make a guy feel like a man!" (When you feel the opposite)
f.   **Non-Verbal Methods**: Refusing to shake hands, glaring at the other person, physically abusing the other

person (e.g., hitting), yawning, ignoring the other person, etc.

Irrational expressions of emotion usually imply that other people have no right to their behavior, that they are bad people for continuing to behave as they do, and that they deserve to be punished. You compound behavior on their part that you do not like with the self-inflicted pain of unpleasant emotions resulting from your irrational beliefs.

Added to self-inflicted pain, in many cases, may be social retaliation. Other people, for rational or irrational reasons of their own, will not appreciate your destructive expression of emotion and may retaliate with some of their own. Then, of course, since they have retaliated so unjustly, you must pay them back—a vicious, destructive circle.

In summary, if you are in an unanticipated situation in which you simply are unable quickly to change your unpleasant feelings, **express** them, but do so rationally. Rational expression of feelings will be in your self-interest because: (1) it will help others understand, and be more understanding of, behavior of yours that may otherwise have been incomprehensible to them; and (2) rational expression of feeling can lead to increased feelings of intimacy between you and these others. (After all, one form of "meaningful," as **versus** "superficial," social interaction is the sharing of deeply held feelings in non-manipulative ways.)

Expressing Likes, Dislikes, Wishes, and Preferences

Person A: "That's the most beautiful painting I have ever seen!"

Person B: (Looking at the same painting) "That's a beautiful painting? Why, I wouldn't wrap my garbage in it!"

Obviously, we have here a case of beauty being in the eye of the beholder. There is nothing good nor bad in this universe, nor anything beautiful or ugly. There are no objective, absolute standards by which these characteristics can be rated; thus, one cannot get evidence to prove that either person A or person B is correct or incorrect. All we can say with any degree of confidence is that person A seems to **like** the painting in question whereas person B seems **not** to like it.

As with paintings, so it is with people (including you). There are no good or bad people in this universe, only fallible humans who do **some** things you like and some you do not like. And it is perfectly natural and rational for you to have your likes, preferences, and wishes. Therefore, there is no reason why you should not communicate your likes and dislikes to others.

And there are many good reasons why you would be better off informing those with whom you choose to live about your preferences. Foremost among these reasons is that, if others know your preferences, they are more likely to do what you like and avoid what you dislike, especially if they believe that you are likely to reciprocate or negotiate a compromise.

As you might have anticipated, there are rational and irrational ways to express preferences. The primary criteria by which the rationality of your preferences may be judged are the same as those for judging an expression of feeling, namely, they are statements of fact, and you are willing to accept responsibility for them. Thus, when you say, "I don't like it when you leave your clothes scattered all over the living room. I would much prefer that you hang them up," you state not only an unarguable fact (the fact is that you don't like it) but you also recognize that your preference is a subjective bias, and that he is not a bad person merely because he failed to act according to your arbitrary expectations. On the other hand, when you say, "You are a sloppy person," the other person can argue, "You're crazy! You call leaving a couple pieces of clothing in the living room sloppy?," and because you have accused him of being a bad person or at least suggested that some of his behavior was bad (sloppy), he may accuse you, albeit irrationally, of being compulsive and of making him angry. Of such stuff are arguments made and friendships broken.

If you wish to live peaceably with others (and you may prefer not to), and if you wish to get the most enjoyment you can out of life (and why not?), by all means let others know the details of your likes and dislikes, for sex, for food, for work, and for anything else important to you. But you would be best off to anticipate that others often will be reluctant or unwilling to behave according to your preferences. That doesn't make them bad—it merely makes them different from you. Accept the differences you find as sometimes unfortunate, often inconvenient, but never awful or terrible. It may be wise for you to search for those whose preferences are as similar or complementary to yours as possible, and to avoid those whose likes and dislikes are incompatible with yours.

When expressing your preferences concerning others' behavior, it is a good idea to use what are called **behavior**

descriptions. "I don't like it when you interrupt me," gives precise information about your preferences, whereas "You are a very rude person" does not. "I like it when you kiss me behind the ear" is more helpful to the other in understanding your likes and dislikes than "You're a fantastic lover!"

Checking Your Perceptions

Suppose that your best friend Suzie walks right by you without saying "Hi," and she has a frightful scowl on her face. Your perception of her behavior at point A might be "Suzie is angry at me." At point C you might feel anxious because at point B you were telling yourself how **awful** it would be if Suzie no longer liked you. In chapter four you were asked to assume the worst at point A, and to go on to point D to dispute the bull you were telling yourself at point B. This can be a good technique, because if you can learn to live comfortably with the worst that can happen, then you can also live with things that are not as bad as you perceived them to be.

However, it is just possible that you have made an error in your perception. It may be that Suzie is indeed angry, but at someone else, and that she is so preoccupied with how she's going to handle the situation that she doesn't even notice you standing there.

The chances are good that you do not have immaculate perception (sorry, but I couldn't resist that). Assuming that your perceptions are not completely accurate, and considering the difficulty of making accurate assessments of the feelings or preferences of others, you would in most cases be wise to check your perceptions before going through a complete ABCD analysis.

Social psychologists have developed the concept of **perception checking** to refer to the act of stating what you perceive to be the inner state of another person. In our example, you would be wise to check your perceptions of Suzie's feelings by saying to her something like, "You seem to be angry at me right now. Am I right?" Or, you might say to Joe, "I'm not sure by the expression on your face whether you're feeling anger or confusion—would you be willing to tell me which?" It is considered to be important when perception checking not to express approval or disapproval of the other's feelings, but to communicate that you wish to understand why they behave as they do.

Suzie may explain to you that she is not angry at you at

all, in which case you have prevented a potential personal problem before it occurs. Most of us tend to perceive what we wish to perceive to some extent, and to find what we are looking for. We would all be best off to check as carefully as we can our perceptions not only of others' feelings but of all potential activating events.

Summary

This chapter concerned itself with presenting techniques that may be useful to you as a supplement to the ABCD approach of the last chapter. It was suggested that: (1) before doing an ABCD analysis, you may benefit from checking your perceptions by means of **perception checking** at point A, (2) after doing an ABCD analysis, and after doing rational-emotive imagery, you may profit from Activity Homework, in which you attempt to deal rationally with those portions of the real world that previously were difficult for you, (3) when it is not possible or practical for you to **control** a strong negative feeling, a good second choice may be to **express** it via a **feeling description**, in which you state accurately how you feel, but in a way that indicates that you are responsible for your own feelings, and (4) it is to your advantage to let others know about your preferences; when your likes and dislikes concern the behavior of others, a good way to communicate your preferences is via **behavior descriptions**, in which you attempt to describe objectively those observable acts of which you approve or disapprove.

Postscript

If you attempt to use this book for your own benefit or for the benefit of someone else, good luck! I would appreciate any feedback, positive or negative, that you would be willing to give me about its effectiveness.

BIBLIOGRAPHY

Ellis, Albert, *Reason and Emotion in Psychotherapy*, 1962, Lyle Stuart, New York.

Ellis, Albert, *How to Live with a Neurotic*, 1969, Award Books.

Ellis, Albert, and Harper, Robert, *A Guide to Rational Living*, 1973 edition, Wilshire Book Company, California.

Maultsby, Maxie C., *Handbook of Rational Self-Counseling or 137 Happiness Habits*, 1971.

Vertes, Robert, "The Should: A Critical Analysis," *Rational Living*, Vol. 6, No. 2, 1971.

Other Books and Materials That May Be of Interest

In addition to his handbook, a number of other materials may be obtained directly from Maxie Maultsby by writing to him at:

Maxie Maultsby, Jr., M.D.
Director Psychiatric OPD
University of Kentucky College of Medicine
Lexington, Kentucky

The Ellis books listed above, as well as many other related books, pamphlets, tape recordings, etc., may be obtained by writing:

Institute for Advanced Study in
Rational Psychotherapy
45 East 65th Street
New York, N.Y. 10021

Appendix A

Rational-Emotive Homework Forms

RATIONAL–EMOTIVE HOMEWORK FORM

When filling out this form, please write legibly. It will be easiest to complete the form correctly if you respond to the sections in this order: C first, then A, then B, and D last.

A. **ACTIVATING EVENT.** Describe your perceptions of the events that "triggered" your emotional upset, e.g., taking a test; your boyfriend telling you he's leaving you for another girl; an acquaintance insulting you, etc.

B. **BELIEFS and Self-Talk About A.** Record what you said to yourself, or what you **must** have said to yourself about the event. Please number each sentence. Examples: 1. **He shouldn't have done that!** 2. **It's awful and I can't stand it!** 3. **He's a very bad person for having done that!**

C. **CONSEQUENCES** of Your Beliefs and Self-Talk. Describe **feelings**, e.g., **anger, fear, depression, guilt.**

D. **DISPUTE Your Beliefs and Self-Talk.** For each sentence in your B section: decide if it is rational (rB) or irrational (iB); explain why it is rational or irrational; and write alternative rational self-talk.

RATIONAL–EMOTIVE HOMEWORK FORM

When filling out this form, please write legibly. It will be easiest to complete the form correctly if you respond to the sections in this order: C first, then A, then B, and D last.

A. **ACTIVATING EVENT.** Describe your perceptions of the events that "triggered" your emotional upset, e.g., taking a test; your boyfriend telling you he's leaving you for another girl; an acquaintance insulting you, etc.

B. **BELIEFS and Self-Talk About A.** Record what you said to yourself, or what you **must** have said to yourself about the event. Please number each sentence. Examples: 1. **He shouldn't have done that!** 2. **It's awful and I can't stand it!** 3. **He's a very bad person for having done that!**

C. **CONSEQUENCES of Your Beliefs and Self-Talk.** Describe **feelings**, e.g., **anger, fear, depression, guilt.**

D. **DISPUTE Your Beliefs and Self-Talk.** For each sentence in your B section: decide if it is rational (rB) or irrational (iB); explain why it is rational or irrational; and write alternative rational self-talk.

RATIONAL–EMOTIVE HOMEWORK FORM

When filling out this form, please write legibly. It will be easiest to complete the form correctly if you respond to the sections in this order: C first, then A, then B, and D last.

A. **ACTIVATING EVENT.** Describe your perceptions of the events that "triggered" your emotional upset, e.g., taking a test; your boyfriend telling you he's leaving you for another girl; an acquaintance insulting you, etc.

B. **BELIEFS and Self-Talk About A.** Record what you said to yourself, or what you **must** have said to yourself about the event. Please number each sentence. Examples: 1. **He shouldn't have done that!** 2. **It's awful and I can't stand it!** 3. **He's a very bad person for having done that!**

C. **CONSEQUENCES of Your Beliefs and Self-Talk.** Describe **feelings**, e.g., **anger, fear, depression, guilt.**

D. **DISPUTE Your Beliefs and Self-Talk.** For each sentence in your B section: decide if it is rational (rB) or irrational (iB); explain why it is rational or irrational; and write alternative rational self-talk.

www.ingramcontent.com/pod-product-compliance
Lightning Source LLC
Chambersburg PA
CBHW071724290326
41933CB00051B/2085